My Dear Cult Leader

Praise for *My Dear Cult Leader*

From reverence to ruin, Aly Acevedo maps the tumultuous terrain of love, loss, and the illusions we build around both. With piercing clarity, these poems lay bare the unspoken violences of intimacy and the strength it takes to reclaim what was lost. *My Dear Cult Leader* is for anyone finding their way back to themselves.

- Sierra DeMulder, *Ephemera*

This book does a thing for which I am simultaneously grateful and resentful: it makes me feel empathy for a horrible man. This book is brimming with empathy, for everyone involved in the cult, and it's Aly's ability to fully illustrate everyone's perspectives that makes her collection stand out. Two lines that I think exemplify that push and pull of evil and humanity are "the power of the ruthless & how lucrative the gentle can be" and "there's no one to pray to when he's made himself the higher power." *My Dear Cult Leader* will teach you a lot, including some things about yourself you didn't want to learn, but I promise you, it will be worth it.

- Neil Hilborn, *About Time*

Aly Acevedo's *My Dear Cult Leader* is an exhilarating journey of self-actualization. With stark clarity, Acevedo exposes the violence of a patriarchal world that seeks to control women's bodies. A cult leader—abusive, seductive—haunts these pages. Though he tries his best to make the speaker small, she refuses that smallness, translating his empty apologies into open meadows. "Tell me I need / a new name," says the speaker in an early address to the cult leader, "& I will forget my own lineage." But the speaker forgets nothing. And she keeps her name, a holy thing, wrenching herself into wholeness. Searing, carnal, true. This is triumphant poetry.

- Josh Tvrdy, *Smut Psalm*

My Dear Cult Leader

poems by

Aly Acevedo

Button Publishing Inc.
Minneapolis
2026

MY DEAR CULT LEADER
POETRY
AUTHOR: Aly Acevedo
COVER DESIGN: Victoria Alvarez

Published by Button Poetry
Minneapolis, MN 55418 | http://www.buttonpoetry.com

◇

Manufactured in the United States of America
PRINT ISBN: 978-1-63834-208-3
EBOOK ISBN: 978-1-63834-140-6

First printing

for Papi—
my first safe place

for Collin—
my sweetest muse

table of contents

four.

five.

My Dear Cult Leader

one.

"dear dear my most distant love—when i dream of you
i wake in a field so blue i drown."
– Danez Smith

we loved each other once

admittedly,
every poem
has become
a study of
how could
you let it go
on that long?
this chemical
love, this
open wound
disregarded
for years.
when i do
remember
you, i watch
myself commit
treason
to my beliefs.
with every
final draft,
i am overwhelmed
with grief.
once, we had it—
i swear.

forgiveness crawls on my lap & asks to stay

i'm nineteen, probably on a pill
i took from someone's cabinet. your name

hasn't touched my lips in months when it lights up
my phone. like a good girl, i undress myself

in my room & wait for your knock.
instead, you ask to talk about that night—

the one i have tried to bury & dispose of.
i call it what it is, *assault.* the heaviest of words,

an aircraft flying nose-first into a field.
you know what you did. though it's been two years,

it still nooses you, still locks your jaw, suffocates
your sleep. that's why you're talking to me,

decorating me in apologies. i stare
at the prescription bottles on my shelf,

the white tissue roses that missed my trash can
& count the divots in my ceiling as you talk.

i forgive you. i forgive you. i forgive you.
the words align with the pattern of my heartbeat.

i forgive you. i forgive you. i forgive you.
i translate your apology into an open meadow,

a relapse of my sweetest drug, an invitation to come back
& see the animal hiding in your closet. my forgiveness,

the green light, a laugh too loud, the gutting of a fish.
i let you crawl inside me again that next summer break.

the cult leader invites you in

everyone must wear red
because that is the color of passion.

braid your hair down your back;
i want to think about whipping you

when i see you. in the morning,
you'll teach the children—i trust

you'll stick to the approved
curriculum. we eat lunch

as a community at noon;
you & i will have a meeting

every tuesday night, alone.
your eyes are so beautiful;

has anyone ever told you that?
as a child, i was a wallflower, broken

& confused just like you. i understand
you more than your family.

i've created all of this
for people like us.

see, i can be gentle. now,
go fix my dinner. i'm hungry.

a new kind of religion

i want to wait to have sex.
your dad calls me a bible beater.
your mom slaps his arm.
i ask you what that means.

your dad calls me a bible beater.
in your basement that night
your fingers wander to the place
on my body that could send me to hell.

in your basement that night,
i talk to you about religion—try to save you.
after our school dance, your friend buys
you a condom at a gas station. we drive home &

i talk to you about religion—try to save you.
you convince me that my body can be your savior.
you unravel me in your hands. ask me
to free you from your virginity.

you convince me that my body can be your savior.
so, i baptize you. forget religion & learn about myself.
learn how i like it, how i don't, learn that i will choose
hell if it means i get carried there by your breath.

so, i baptize you. forget religion & learn about myself.
learn that i will allow your tongue to negotiate every conviction.
i think you knew too. how you didn't even flinch when i said
i want to wait to have sex.

nine years later

now, he lives in the town where i was born.
halfway across the country from where

he turned his body into a whip.
my forgiveness has carved a home

in my opinion of him.
i'm a selfish poet, dancing around truth

like a ballerina in her final act.
let me say it straight: my high school sweetheart

raped me the day before he left.
upstairs, his mother was in the kitchen

putting the dishes away, her crockpot seething.
in any dark room, i can feel his hands

pressing me into his couch.
the same hands that i let hold me

while i slept. i've spent nine years living
with the hole he shaped in me.

when i close my eyes, i rewatch our episodes
on my eyelids: my blue prom dress, his glasses,

the basement—always the basement—
his hands, again, & how i laid there so still.

claimed property

the day my parents declared divorce
was the first time i ever took a full breath.

before, i thought marriage was just staying
in the living room of dissatisfaction.
before, i would yell from my bedroom for a
ceasefire, so i could sleep in silence.

i learned love from their best attempts at it.
my dad tells me that there was a time when
they were a team.

but all i can remember is the day they brought out
all the appliances, plates & pots from their cabinet
homes & went back & forth claiming which item would
come live with them in their new separate homes.

i choose the toaster. i'm taking all the coffee mugs.
i want whatever will chisel a hole into your body.
what can i strip from your familiarity to make
you remember me every time you need it?

the cult leader as a child

at the age of four, he sat down at a piano, started playing
& never stopped. his favorite songs to play were christmas carols
because they just make people happy.

by seven, he coordinated a club with the neighborhood boys,
to join you had to ding dong ditch a neighbor of his choosing—
most of the time, he chose the man returned from war
in the blue house who always came outside with his gun.
he liked to watch fear stain across his peers, how they ran to him,
pulsing & obedient.

in middle school, he learned he loved acting
in plays. any character on command. the audience engulfed
in every word; his pacing, perfection, his tears, how they could swallow
him whole, then disappear within seconds.

puberty favored him, deepened his voice to a seductive velvet.
but when he was sixteen, he watched his father drunkenly wilt his
mother, seven purple flowers on her face. it was that night that he met
their beloved heirlooms: his father's violence, his mother's allegiant
heart. the power of the ruthless & how lucrative the gentle can be.

having a panic attack on the highway

the road is so lonely at this hour.
darkness holds me in its fathomless arms.

the only destination in mind is wherever

i can find peace in your absence—which means
i'm aimlessly looking for you behind every tree

& road sign while knowing you are four states away.

every song on the radio becomes about you,
every mile marker is just the date of your birth.

my tears blur my vision, so i pull over,

stumble my way onto the grass by the road.
fall to my knees & scream at the rolling hills—

its peace no match for my ultraviolence.

i grab fistfuls of dirt just to throw it back at itself,
transform into a feral animal yelping at the moon,

the despondence pulses in me until the panic

succumbs to its klonopin god. my body crawls
back into the front seat. like an addict,

my thumb types your name into my phone.

right before i click call, it slips
onto my floorboard. i follow the thought

of you back home.

i love you, my dear cult leader

now that i am beautiful, since you told me i am,
i look in the mirror every morning

just to stare at the freckles on my shoulders.
i grab my stretch marks & admire the roads

they have paved. the nights i spend
in your bed are the closest i have ever been

to wholeness, holiness. i know
your fascination with crystals

& liquor. your shoulders, how tense
they are until my hands stroke them.

don't you see how every part of you
is the most interesting part of me?

you ask me how loyal i am & i think
of the stories i heard once on the TV.

the headlines meant to isolate those
with purpose from those stuck in some

independence illusion. so, i say to you,
tell me you want to brand me & i will

stoke the fire myself. tell me i need
a new name & i will forget my own lineage.

for the rest of my life, i won't let go.
i'm irrevocably, eternally yours.

nobody wants to develop my negatives in their dark room.

– Desireé Dallagiacomo

CLASSIFIED SECTION

Wisteria News

CLASSIFIED SECTION

YOU NEED A DEAR ~~CULT~~ LEADER

feel like you don't belong? spent years trying to find yourself? stuck in the same routine?

well, it sounds like you need a community of like-minded individuals who all follow the same charismatic **leader**!

our dear ~~cult~~ leader at the wisteria commune is the perfect person to help all your problems fade away.

our *family* is committed to sharing our message & breathing newness into this tiresome life.

we value our community & none of us are adrift– *at least not anymore*.

does this sound like a fit for you?

attend a seminar, **we would love to** enlighten **you** further.

head on down to the wisteria commune, where we can promise a **BETTER** quality of life!

side effects of a dear ~~cult~~ leader may include manipulation, isolation & disconnection from family members. you may experience signs of emotional, cognitive, financial & psychological abuse. extreme cases have resulted in dissociation, suicidal ideation & encouragement to commit harm to yourself & others.

when i was seventeen

we took a class trip to a conference in minneapolis. it was the year my hair grew to my waist. the month when the word prom dripped from my mouth hourly. in the hotel elevator, a man three times my age asked why there were so many kids at the hotel. i smiled, told him about the school trip. the elevator doors opened like a bottle of wine. as i watched everyone spill out of it, a strong arm pulled me back. i felt the lashing of the man's hand as he clenched parts of my body. the grunt in my ear, the hard feeling from his zipper, how he floated off the elevator & didn't start running until i yelled for help. three hours later, the police called my teacher & i to come identify him; he was caught trying to take off another teenage girl's swimsuit in the hotel pool. when i saw him, handcuffed to a chair, (no metaphor here) he licked his lips & growled at me. it was this night that fear nested in me, declared my mind the perfect home to live out its wildest fantasies. instead of pressing charges, police kicked him out of the hotel. no one asked me how i was, instead ice skated around my misfortune or gawked as their words failed them. for years after, i avoided elevators, decided i would climb twenty flights of stairs if it meant no one could touch me.

i can't make this up

& you wanna know some shit?
i met him, the one who shaped a hole in me,
on that same school trip to minneapolis.
within one day of knowing i existed,
he heard the rumors of the old man
assaulting me in the elevator. said nothing,
instead haloed me with worthiness
as he pulled me into a photobooth to take
four photos to remember, glided his fingers
to interlock with mine & waited when he wanted
to kiss me. fast forward six months, still seventeen,
still succumbing to unsolicited hands—this time, his.

the cult leader's first love

her ethereal beauty clung to his body like ivy, trapped every inch
of his attention until all his thoughts dangled forever in front of him.

his desire made an animal of him. he called her twice a night, slept

with a picture of her underneath his pillow & threatened every male
lab partner & childhood friend. when she said *i love you*, he'd ask her

to state specific qualities she admired. the way she recited his perfection

back to him is what made him love her the most. when she broke up
with him, he waited outside her work for a week. after she kept

saying no, his scent still showed up in her sheets, the bathroom window

suspiciously remained unlocked every morning. he cried
in every interrogation, lied & said it was because he missed her.

the semester we all were afraid

kansas state university, fall 2017

call your roommates as you walk home from class,
lock your doors at night, check your windows twice.
the police call him the kansas state rapist, no one can catch him.
three sorority girls assaulted in their parking lots.

lock your doors at night, check your windows twice.
i woke to a man watching me sleep last week.
three sorority girls assaulted in their parking lots,
another house was broken into down the street.

i woke to a man watching me sleep last week,
i moved my taser underneath my pillow.
another house was broken into down the street.
why isn't the university acknowledging this?

i moved my taser underneath my pillow,
asked my landlord for new locks on my door.
why isn't the university acknowledging this?
their entire female student body is suffocating in fear.

asked my landlord for new locks on my door,
the total is twelve women attacked, five houses broken into.
their entire female student body is suffocating in fear.
we've been listening when our friends say

the total is twelve women attacked, five houses broken into,
all women attacked have been in sororities.
we've been listening when our friends say
call your roommates as you walk home from class

& nothing about *him*.

the man in the darkened room

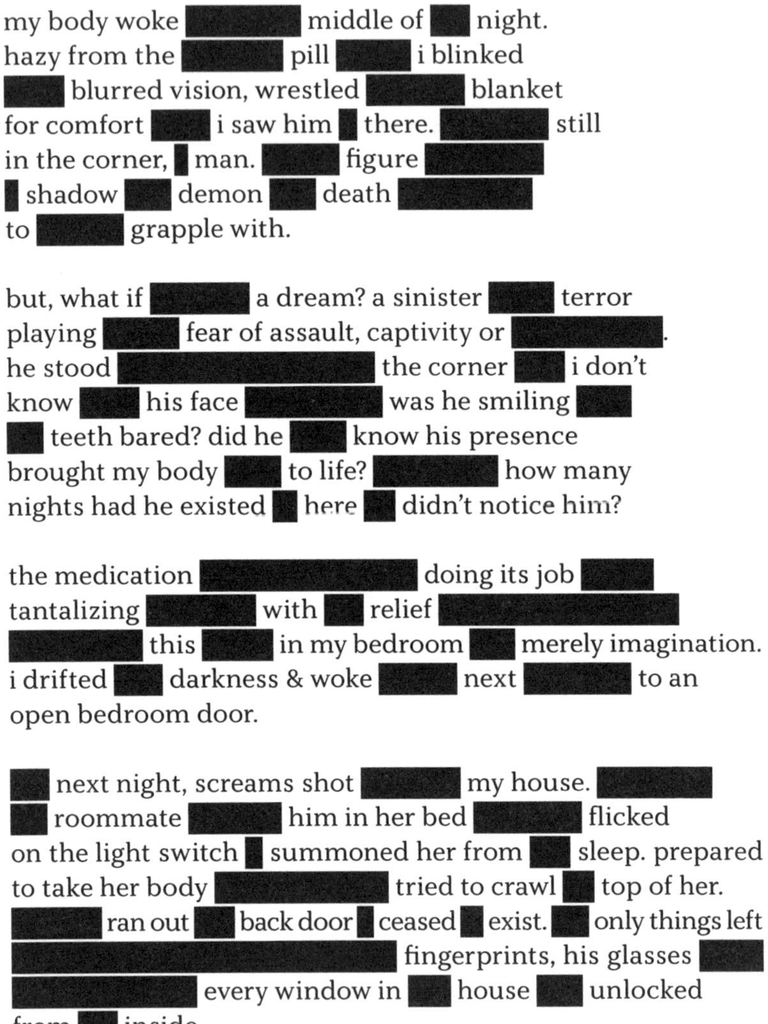

my body woke middle of night.
hazy from the pill i blinked
blurred vision, wrestled blanket
for comfort i saw him there. still
in the corner, man. figure
shadow demon death
to grapple with.

but, what if a dream? a sinister terror
playing fear of assault, captivity or .
he stood the corner i don't
know his face was he smiling
teeth bared? did he know his presence
brought my body to life? how many
nights had he existed here didn't notice him?

the medication doing its job
tantalizing with relief
this in my bedroom merely imagination.
i drifted darkness & woke next to an
open bedroom door.

next night, screams shot my house.
roommate him in her bed flicked
on the light switch summoned her from sleep. prepared
to take her body tried to crawl top of her.
ran out back door ceased exist. only things left
fingerprints, his glasses
every window in house unlocked
from inside.

your mother's house in tennessee

we sit in the living room waiting for his mother
to arrive home. i am four years older
than her last sight of me. i stare at the decorations

that line the walls of her new home & feel estranged.
as i wait, i recall every conversation we had while she cooked,
every dream where i would mistake her for my own mother.

when she walks through the door, her face stains with confusion
until he says my name. *i didn't recognize you with blonde hair, sweetie.*
we spend the afternoon outside, recollecting the lost time—

how she moved to tennessee after the divorce, how i have my first
apartment. when he left to grab us more beer, she looked at me
so directly & said *he loves you, but he isn't ready for you.*

at the end of the night, she yelled to him, *i like her,*
don't mess this up again. when he said he wouldn't,
i believed him. i truly, faithfully did.

the first tuesday night with my dear cult leader

i want to get to know you, the real you.
take a deep breath. you're safe with me.

i don't respond, so you inch closer.
i stare into your gentle green eyes
& feel as if i'm suspended in air.
i tell you about my family:
their grudges, unforgiving as winter.
how i'm incapable of their holy pardon.
my eyes well with tears, your arms
guide me to lay in your lap, your fingers
glide over my skin & you hum a slow song
i don't recognize. the words felt so tender,
the genesis of our eden, an open gate inviting me
in. you, servant heart, so benevolent, i was meant
to find you. you lean in to kiss me. my body swells,
my breathing shifts.

i'll worship you perpetually.

three.

"if you listened to my chest it would sound like
a river ice breakup, like i just learned how to breathe."
– Kyla Jamieson

my dear cult leader, we all talk

the day Daisy stepped onto the compound,
i watched your pupils dilate into greedy mirrors.
the next day, Cassie told me Daisy snuck home

with lipstick smeared onto her chin,
her perfect blonde hair disheveled. everyone
heard your moans whimper across our empty land.

on sunday, i watched Daisy fold laundry.
all the hues of red creasing in her hands—
she doesn't even know it's your favorite color.

the women whispered to me at lunch
he called her beautiful.
i didn't finish my food because i know she is.

but my dear, it's tuesday, the night i get to lay
in your bed. i enter through the back door, disrobe
myself, unfold like a centerfold on your bed.

i hear your feet as they hit the steps, my heartbeat
thumping from my legs. you push the door open,
her hand in yours. *i think Daisy should join us tonight.*

when i say no, you tell her to undress in the bathroom,
grab my cheeks in your rough hands. *who are you truly rejecting?*
tell me the first memory you felt shame. how clever you must be

to know how to twist me into obedience. Daisy joins us
& only you enjoy. i run straight to Cassie to tell her what you did.

every poem has become about my body

all the girls in seventh grade paraded their
new bodies around. with foam in my mouth, i envied them.

studied them. prayed for at least B-cups.
looked longingly in my bedroom mirror. when would i bloom?

i wanted to be the reason boys looked
twice, the distraction in english class, a dream unobtainable.

my sequined shirts were never pressured
by curves, my training bra became my biggest shame.

my innocence intertwined with
prayers & waiting. *dear genetics,* *let it be my turn soon.*

:::

tonight,
i want to mourn
each increased
cup size
& beckon my
naivety back.
before,
sexual assault
wasn't a word
in my vocabulary.
now, it is
a shadow that
follows me.
every poem
has become
about my body.

as if i am still
blaming it
for what has
happened.
as if figure
had any part
in fate
at all.

after ripping my tampon

legs straddled & angled to the ceiling.
tears
welled. fell.
inside me, metal scraping, fingers
excavating. emergency
room. hours ago, pulled my tampon out. it
ripped. searched my insides.
all i pulled was more blood.
blood on my toilet.
on the floor.
in my fingernails.

now, so many hands are
stretching searching finding nothing.

now, i am back on his couch.
giving hurting feeling nothing.

now, i am in his room.
begging shaking becoming nothing.

they asked me if i have a history of sexual violence. yes.

told me everything they were doing
yet still i don't trust them.
yet still it is his hands.
yet still i'm on my back.

so sorry, sweetie. we are almost done. breathe. you're doing so well.
you're going to feel a pulling sensation. i have to open you more to see.
we can't find anything.
you're safe to put a tampon in again.

the cult leader convinces you to stay

doubt is only as powerful as you make it.
what i'm saying is your desire to leave

is simply a distraction. you ran away

from your old life for a reason,
do you really want to go back?

do you think your family would love you

after they know what you've done?
you swore your devotion to me.

a vow as final as a funeral pyre.

i chose you, picked you
straight from the vine, how could you

leave a place where you're so cherished?

i can't find magic in remembering

i click my heels three times, say *i'm healed. i'm healed. i'm healed.* but no wizard appears. i borrow a book of spells from the library, enchant myself to fall for strangers on the street, but every person

looks back at me with *his* eyes. i can't find magic in remembering, so give me a potion to take, initiate me into the witches' coven, i'll be the most observant apprentice or hopeless test subject.

i'll be as loyal as i was to him, i promise. the day we met, a woman read our tarot cards, said we were going to be in each other's lives for a long time; i just didn't know she meant like this.

what are your intentions, my dear cult leader

in public, you tell us to love, to spread your teachings & grow
the community. but nobody knows

of the empty liquor bottles littered on your bedroom floor
or the guns you have living

in your basement. you're a coiled snake ready to burst its jaws open
& i've become your constant alibi.

please, don't punish me, but i can't sleep next to you & not know
the visions within you.

you once led with open palms, now an iron fist,
erratic as a landslide. i'm suffocating

in my allegiance. is power your foible? who are you becoming?
what are you making of us?

la llorona speaks

after Olivia Gatwood & Reed Bobroff

sometimes, i hear the boys walk past the river as they howl my name, *la llorona*. like i am a dare or a dagger to dance with. their tongues roll the letters to my name. i imagine each of them as my husband.

:::

his skin was like honey. sometimes,
i wish my skin still sticky. instead,
my hands prune in the mucky river.

the water brings back the memory,
i wish to abandon... i loved them—
i mean him. i mean—

i smelled her perfume on his collar,
so i tore it off of him. washed away
that cheap elixir he didn't know existed.

in the morning, i served him breakfast.
asked our children to kiss him goodbye,
look what our love can make.

i still imagine their faces.
our daughter would be six tomorrow,
our son, nine. they visit me in damp sleep.

the next night,
my husband came home with lipstick
on his neck. scratches on his back.

what kind of banshee was he making love to?
what kind of monster did he want to make of me?
i grabbed our children by the wrist.
untied their shoes.

i hear they washed up on shore two days later.
lo siento, mi bebés.
i hear my husband sobbed in our vacant home.
good.

i live in the woods now. leeches drink off my back,
mold growing under my fingernails, mud & bugs in my hair.
i hear voices come from the tree line & weep

mis hijos. *mis hijos.*
mis hijos.
mis hijos. *mis hijos.*
mis hijos. *mis hijos.*
mis hijos.

mis hijos. *mis hijos.* *mis hijos.* *mis hijos.*
mis hijos. *mis hijos.*

they're never there. sometimes, i wait
for my husband to come. i can feel his whispered
i love you undressing me... but i always smell *her* perfume.

:::

the boys are walking by the river again. taunting me. *la llorona. la llorona.* how easily i can name them *husband* or *child.* it's all the same to me. i could drown their youth, too. let their bodies wash ashore, so my husband knows i am still alive.

i'll write you as my villain, but once you were my god

i remember your hands, how they lived on my thighs,
how they'd inevitably retreat, only to be followed by lies.

the quarterly *i still love you's* that would caress my doubt.
i wish i could have believed i was better without.

i want to say that we were young, that we didn't know better,
but we grew into our twenties, still chained together.

i'll write you as my villain, but once you were my god.
entangled my worth to your kaleidoscope facade.

now, i cower in the palms of love as if all i can ever be is left
& you live some bewildered life, free from your theft.

tell me, are you just hopelessly depraved?
just between us, how are you so unscathed?

it's always the same these days

i'm aging in a bar in el paso, texas
when you attempt to pull my body

through the phone. like a tulip, i emerge
from your dirt. bright, dainty, temporary.

it's always the same these days—
i've missed you, i love you, i won't leave again.

however, i'm drunk in the desert
& the only love in this city is a bartender

with a name i can't pronounce
at the moment. so, i sink another

shot & slur *happy new year's baby*—
a kiss bouncing between time zones,

a calamitous conquest. in the mood
of midnight, i feel masochistic.

why should we draw out the battle?
go sharpen your teeth, give me a snarl.

i'll pull out the tissues, the hollow *fuck you's.*
give me your worst this time.

none of it matters anyway,
i just love to want you at this point.

four.

"i finally found my rhythm when i realized
that even the steps backward were part of the dance."
– Melody Godfred

in favor of my desires

after Kim Addonizio

bring me a raspberry lemonade
& the crispiest of bacon—the closer
to burnt, the better. i want all
the clingy cats in this city
sleeping in my bed tonight.
or new silk white sheets will do.
give me a bowl of indica with a bowl
of fruity pebbles. i like my mind
weightless after a long day.
oh, the birds, let all of them build
their nests on my deck. i will guard
the eggs as if they were my kin;
give mama bird some rest.
play all the reality dating shows
on a loop—i know they never end
up together, but let me cry, let me
believe for a moment they'll make it.
when i cry, let the water
bubble down my cheeks until
it soaks the collar of my shirt—
it probably needs to be washed anyway.
i am a lump in the throat,
the wrong meal that you refuse
to tell the waiter they served you,
the shopping bags left in your trunk
that you bring in when your husband
is asleep. spent so much time concerned
with opinions of others, i sacrificed
all the desires my dreams painted.
so, give me the longest of showers,
the permission to not smile at everyone
walking on the street. i want the world
to beckon to my snap, which reminds me—
why isn't my lemonade here, yet?

the night the power went out

a month from our two-year anniversary
in the stagnant heat of summer,

a storm commanded our city to bend
to its temper, & in the dark, we ate

each other whole on top of our comforter.
sweat paraded down our backs,

the thunder lured our primal, a hunger
that sinewed us together. the food in our fridge

softening, all the clocks dead;
the only electricity in the city beaming

from our bodies. i looked at you
through the haze of candlelight

& for a second, i could have sworn
we'd become the sun.

it was midnight in michigan

the boy with enough stories to put a sailor to shame
placed a small, square piece of paper on my tongue.
i didn't come here for this, but i couldn't
deny anything he dangled in front of me—
a tab, his body, a promise that he would
text me back after i flew home.
when it hit, i was on the toilet
watching fairies fly around.
i couldn't remember how to control
my body until he said my name through the door.
when i laid down, i watched skulls float,
made peace with death.
curled my body into a fetus—
he, my womb. awaited a new birth,
but he was on more tabs than me,
his arms might as well have been rope.
but i clung to them. draped them over
my body like a sash. whispered *we are such bad poets.*
(& we were then: orchestrating words
we couldn't keep, looking up at the sky
when we talked because we were too nervous
to look each other in the face, buying plane tickets
just to write a few lines on the back of them.
i don't regret him. he told me he loved me
in an uncontrollable, unfortunate way
& i told him, in the end, i hoped it was him.)
when the sun began to rise, we went to the basement
to hide from it. found our friend talking
to the brick wall. we sat in a circle,
turned on the radio & the mushroom man
poster on the wall sang to me—*look at the stars,*
look how they shine for you. the instrumental hit
& with it, the feeling of never wanting to leave
this house. three months before this night,
i had switched schools because i was suicidal,

had taken so many substances, i applied to be
in the white lighter club. but that night saved me.
that boy looked at me through his jimmy hendrix
sunglasses like i was a galaxy's dream, my body
a supernova. i lived as a star for a mere
twelve hours. i don't know that boy in michigan
anymore, don't know what his stories sound like,
but when that song comes on, i'm there again.
living in that basement, three fold-out chairs,
the universe living in our hallucinations.

somewhere, yes

after Danez Smith

a midnight full moon leaks
        into open windows in my room.
the knives are tucked to bed
        in drawers. the front door is unlocked
& i am sleeping unbothered
        by all of this. there is no true crime.
no women murdered because of
        what they were wearing
or who they didn't talk to.
        no women left dismembered
on isolated hiking trails
        or bodies uncovered
behind dumpsters on college campuses.
        here, there is no language
for *murder* or *rape*. here, it is night
        all the time. i've memorized
every constellation. i go on walks alone
        with headphones to bask in the moonlight.
please, don't beckon me back to your world.
        i cannot bear it anymore.
i cannot live in fear & consider
        my life well spent.

the cult leader has a panic attack

for an hour, the cult leader talks about gentleness. through love,
we can find ourselves. through ourselves, we can change the world.
a standing ovation ensues after his speech. he looks to his followers,

their clothes dyed to his favorite color, the women who loyally weave
their hair into a sexual fantasy, how they believe they have found god—
or better. he feels his heart roaring *imposter, imposter, imposter.* he runs

to the bathroom, splashes water on his face, demanding breath
into dominance. he falls to his knees in desperation, only to realize
there's no one to pray to when he's made himself the higher power.

ode to my period

there is nothing subtle about showing up all at once, thicker than syrup
seeping through my panties. the *not pregnant* party has arrived
& you apologize for being late, again. but i am so delighted
you made it. now, instead of crying alone, i get to cry in company.
now, i burn an extra 100 calories a day. who needs a workout
when i have you—the unfertilized egg swindler, gutting the harp
of my uterus, playing your favorite song. most men can't look
you in your face, let alone touch the river you baptize me in.
how i can envy you sometimes. i, too, wish to be so unapologetically
myself that no rejection or judgment will deter me from my truth.
i'm sorry i hated you for so long—those months i'd wished
you didn't come, the negative tests in my trash can, the parade of tears
marching down my face. i was wrong to define you as an unjust ruler
when all you are is my flesh. you're the loudest, most destructive
one at the party, but the one i miss most when you've gone.

let me be timeless, just once

after Olivia Gatwood

i have an irrational belief that being a poet & owning an iPhone
can't coexist. i cut lines in poems referring to technology

as if i am not using a laptop to write to begin with.

i read Mary Oliver at night & envy the way her poems
dance between decades. there's something timeless about

the changing of seasons or how animals can become metaphors

for our own human need to let go. i met my husband on a dating app.
in the morning, my phone shrieks for attention & i give it

without hesitation. reader, if i can't be perennial, let me pretend

just for a second: it is summer & my skin drinks sunlight.
it is summer & the bugs drink my sweet elixir. how lucky we are

to all depend on each other. life would stop if we lost our cycle.

the blue jay sits on a branch outside my patio & squawks
for the bird feeder to be refilled. once satisfied, it returns to the

branch to let me admire its beauty as a thank you. i am abundant

because another being knows i am alive. i am timeless
simply because i have helped another survive.

killing us

a golden shovel after Charles Bukowski

my sweet tennessee whiskey, for
you, i once abandoned all
rationale based off things
like half-assed texts or *soon we will*
be back together propaganda. i would kill

whoever was in my bed & wait for you.
then a full moon would come again. both
a siren song & a signal that we were slowly
waning away from each other again &
again. i lived in that cycle. your fastly

changing allegiances, my leech-like tendencies. but,
the last trip i saw you, i told myself *it's*
not going to work. it's too much.
so, i devoted four final days. better
known as my last plea for matrimony. to

live without you felt so foreign, i be-
came scared i killed
us in the name of nothing. a year flew by
& you attempted a revival. but by then, you'd become a
ghost story i laughed about with my new lover.

my place in autumn

the water runs like a violin,
the trees guard this place like a secret,

the parrotfeather weeds line the rocks around the pond.

my body lightens as the wind caresses my face.
i call this place *my place* because i want to believe

i'm the only one who has written poems on this land.

in my dreams, i elope here.
my lover sits next to me while the carcasses

of plants blow in the bitter wind. the trees breathe,

as we hear the silence that is only
broken by the birds chirping, i lean in & whisper,

this is the place that healed me, where i ran when i didn't have you.

five.

"how we have managed our way to this bed—
beholden to heat like dawn indebted to light."
– Nicole Sealey

if i got another chance at it

after Ollie Schminkey

i declare that if i could live my life again,
knowing i would end up in Collin's arms,

        i wouldn't change anything.

i'd write notes to myself
that encouraged me to follow

        all the ruinous impulses.

lead myself to each depressive episode,
set up a breadcrumb trail

        to *that* other man's house,

say the words, *he must be the one,*
knowing damn well what's to come.

        i would rent the apartment next door

just to hear my cries through the wall.
i'd applaud every misstep, leave flowers at my door

        after each heartbreak,

give praise to all the boys
as i kill them off my plotline.

        i want all the pain to bruise me

from the inside out. just for
the moment of relief i will get

        the first time my love sleeps beside me.

you message me *my family wanted me to tell you hello.*

i stare at my screen & decode each word.

my

dear, i've missed the house we used to play in.
your quiet has led me into a forest of my own regret.
save me. i'm a victim of all my decisions.

family

is still asking about you. i show up to every gathering
empty handed. they say your name
& i have to tell them you're married now.

wanted

to tell you i'm sorry, my most practiced sport.
historically, your achilles heel.

me

& my guilt will live in your inbox until you're ready.
let me pull you back into me, if only for a second.
give me your pinkest of cheeks, the single freckle
on your lips.   i am on my knees.

to

be honest, i still don't know if i can trust my intentions.
you've become my sweetest ritual. june comes, then suddenly
i see your face in all the strangers on the street.

tell

me you still love me. even if it is somewhere deep & hidden.
a diary page that you've burned. give me something.
i just have to believe that all these years weren't built
in the name of nothing.

you

are visiting me in my dreams again. i cradle your body, try to learn all the new parts of you. *tell me your favorite song. what book is keeping you up at night?* i wake to an empty room & mourn you .

hello.

ode to the mundane

this is a poem for the *i made it* texts,
the clock on our stove we change twice a year,
how making the bed is easier when done by two.
how i love the way you season food,
our whiteboard calendar where we leave notes—
like when i told you alliteration is my favorite
literary tool & the next day you wrote
Aly ate ass & told me how hard it was
to come up with three simple words.
this is a poem for the moment i finish
writing & run to the living room
to read you my first drafts. an ode
to every toothbrush that has lived in our bathroom,
the occasions we intentionally wear matching clothes
or how i tie my hair back every time i eat in bed.
the way you always let me take a corner bite of
your rangoons because i love the crunch, not the crab.
our chosen shows we fall asleep to: *rick & morty,*
family guy, archer. & how can i forget
every shower where i have talked to you
through the door, the appreciation you give me
when i lay out your clothes for the next day
or how much joy you show when you refill
the bird feeder. proof that we have enough visitors
to go through a bag biweekly. O, the sweet, mundane
moments we make routine of. how lucky we are
that we moved in together within months
& still celebrate the minutes. here's to shared bills,
how your legs always find me in your sleep,
the three animals we are raising & how every note
i write you ends with *love you 'til i die.*

this poem is about sex

it will not be a story of a body being stolen this time.
strangers won't look at me with horror in their eyes.

no *i'm so sorry that happened to you.* instead, let me paint
your mind with permission & pleasure. my man

brushes his fingertips down my thighs, pulling
goosebumps from their graves. instead, i kiss his neck

over & over until that metronome is reinvented
with our hips. i don't care if the neighbors hear tonight,

let consent descend into the breeze. this time, my hands
explore. this time, we finish & our giggles float

to the ceiling, spin around the fan & bounce off the walls
while we hold each other—exposed, naked, like no one

& nothing has ever existed outside of the empire
of our bodies.

tonight, we float

tonight, there will not be any sadness in the sky.

put on your favorite shoes,

i will grab my sacred pink hair clip.

tuck peonies behind our ears—i heard they are in season.

drink water straight from the stream.

a little dirt won't hurt when we are trying to grow.

walk with me until we find the clearest view of the stars.

claim a constellation or make up a new one.

i do it all the time.

pass me the joint, join me as i float.

watch as a solar flare stretches its arms so south,

the kansas sky burns.

i am enamored by my hope in the universe.

yes, i realize how dramatic it is to say *the universe,*

but i just want to see something beautiful

& believe it's meant just for us—the misunderstood lovers.

O, holy aurora.
O, dancing light.

i want to be you when i grow up.

i fantasize about being so vivid with life,

that someone drives to a field,

lays out a blanket

& escapes into my beauty.

whatever lives after this lifetime

in this lifetime, we play board games on saturday nights,
drink spring water & kiss in sets of three. in the next, i am a waitress
serving you dinner & you complain to a manager about my service.

we never see each other again. the next, you are my first
one-night-stand. in the next, you hit my car during rush hour, next,
you're my children's pediatrician, next, i'm your wife's best friend.

next, we don't find each other. the end of our lives become a stop motion
movie, a desperate longing pulling us into our next rotation.
in our last minutes, recollection floods our cerebellums,

memories, forgotten, string together like christmas lights
before the final dark. in the next lifetime, we rashly trade virginities
at sixteen, bear no children, instead, spend eighty years

trying to memorize what was once lost. whatever lives after this lifetime,
i want to depart together, even if we never learn each other's new names
or ever breathe a shared breath. when death inevitably carries us,

fear will not brim in me. i will walk into that blissful void
knowing that nothing lasts forever, except the chance
of another existence with you.

your finest hour

after Sierra DeMulder & Sharon Olds

if you've truly bestowed upon me your finest hour,
	i have nothing else to mourn.

you are a grave i no longer have to visit out of guilt.
	i've made peace with our death.

which is to say, i have stopped wondering what it was
	like to be in love with me. what wrongdoing

was i always committing? if i heard your voice now,
	it would be as unrecognizable as static.

no longer are you the anchor holding me in rough seas.
	instead, a shipwreck i have survived.

it's not that you are a heinous storm, it's that you are
	the reason all my petals fell to the ground.

if all those years were your most moving performance,
	then no matter what starring role

i lived, the last act was always going to be silent.
	jaws wired shut.

goodbye, my dear cult leader

it is june & i am leaving you for the fifth time.

before, i spent days wrapped around your finger, now i don't know
what parts of me you invented & which personality fragments

i should learn to hate. your voice plays on a loop in my dreams.
in my consciousness, your voice is the silence.

sometimes, i don't think the world is beautiful without you
there to tell me it is. i'm trying to forget you

without burning our whole home down. this is the hardest goodbye,
simply because i know it must be the last.

crown shyness

a phenomenon where tree canopies do not touch to avoid disease & provide sunlight to the lower branches.

ten years have moved through me

& i'm still teaching myself how to be unbothered

when i hear your name. i thought i'd be bound to you,

permanent as a scar, loyal to counterfeit sweet nothings.

instead, i am writing in my backyard & i see us

in the trees—their canopies never touching at the top,

survival more significant than contact. we've made it out

of each other's blight, sashayed onto opposite

sides of the country, repressed any acknowledgement

that our roots will always drink the same soil.

i've become the gentlest version of me, in love

with another man & my wounds have taught me

that i'll never know what someone else is living through.

so, i'm extending this poem to you. a peace offering

laced with the recognition that you never got it right

with me, but i still believe good has entwined with your heart.

i'm picturing you, remarkably refreshed, an open road

that wasn't paved in time for me.

button poetry

acknowledgements

Sierra DeMulder - thank you for creating an environment where this manuscript could come alive. you were the first poet i ever saw perform & from that moment on i knew i wanted to build a life around this art form. you have always been an inspiration to me but the fact that you edited this manuscript makes the journey all the more meaningful.

Nadia Sabalu-Hadl - thank you for being my best friend, for celebrating me always & for consistently affirming that my poetry dreams were worth chasing.

Logan Stacer - thank you for taking the time to read early drafts of these poems & offer your insight. you are a light in the kansas city art community & i am grateful to have called you a friend all these years.

Darren Epping Fuentes, Craig Brown, Dan Cutter, Cassidy Stefka-Emmerich, Delta Wilson, Jacob Miller-Klugesherz & Roger Steen - wow! college speech changed my life & each of you guided me through that journey. you nurtured my love of poetry & performance & supported me unwaveringly even through the most difficult seasons of my life. the kansas state university speech program laid the foundation for poems like *la llorona speaks* & *it was midnight in michigan.* i'm so grateful there were no off-limit ideas. thank you for giving my creativity a home.

Carolyn Cook - i'm forever grateful for the time i spent in your forensics program at lansing high school. it was in your class that i first discovered my love for performing. i wouldn't be the writer or performer i am today without your early guidance & encouragement.

the late Danielle Perry - while writing this book i couldn't wait to include your name in these acknowledgments. it was in your class that i wrote a poem for the first time. you pushed me, encouraged me & helped me submit to my first contest. you were the first person to tell me you believed i could publish a book one day. i hope your soul is resting somewhere beautiful. i'm so grateful that you were here once.

Dr. Matthew Guelker - thank you for being in my corner—not only as a therapist but as a friend—since i was nineteen. i'm fortunate to have had your voice shaping my growth & lifting me up along the way.

Papi - it is not lost on me how fortunate i am to have a father like you. thank you for your sacrifice—coming to the united states at such a young age & working tirelessly so that your children could have a better life. it means everything to know you're proud of me. i'm glad your poetry gene found its way to me.

Nito (Carlos Jr.) & Cole - i am endlessly thankful to call you my brothers. every step of my life has included your fierce love & support. thank you for being my constants in every season.

Aba, Abuelo, Titi, Tio Beau, Tio Jamie, Ericka, Juno (Beau Jr.), Marisa, Jaime, Jael, Liliana - i love our puerto rican family with all my heart. thank you for your unrelenting love & encouragement.

Collin - thank you for loving me so gently, for holding my trauma with care & for showing me—every day—that i am worthy of a good true love. this book wouldn't have its soft ending without you. i'll love you 'til i die.

to the entire Button Poetry Team - thank you for believing in not just this book but in me. it has been an absolute dream to join this community through your incredible support.

to all the poets, friends & family who have shaped the way i write - thank you. your presence is in every line.

& lastly, **to the reader** - thank you for supporting the arts, for trusting my writing 'til the end. the world is a kinder place with you in it.

all my love.

acknowledgements continued

thank you to the following publishers for providing a home for earlier drafts of these poems from this collection:

Anti-Heroin Chic: "nine years later" & "every poem has become about my body"

TRASH MAG: "somewhere, yes"

resources

RAINN (Rape, Abuse & Incest National Network)

1-800-656-HOPE (4673)

English: www.rainn.org

Español: www.rainn.org/es

National Sexual Violence Resource Center (NSVRC)

www.nsvrc.org

National Domestic Violence Hotline

1-800-799-SAFE (7233) | Text "START" to 88788

www.thehotline.org

National Teen Dating Abuse Helpline

1-866-331-9474 | Text "LOVEIS" to 22522

www.loveisrespect.org

Crisis Text Line

Text "HOME" to 741741

StrongHearts Native Helpline

1-844-762-8483

www.strongheartshelpline.org

Esperanza United

www.esperanzaunited.org

Asian Pacific Institute on Gender-Based Violence (API-GBV)

www.api-gbv.org

Restore Forward

www.restoreny.org/black-womens-blueprint/

Metropolitan Organization Countering Sexual Assault (MOCSA)

816-531-0233

www.mocsa.org

1in6 - Male Identifying Sexual Assault Support Groups

www.1in6.org

about the author

Aly Acevedo is a Puerto Rican and Vietnamese poet, educator and speaker based in the Kansas City area. Her debut collection, *My Dear Cult Leader* (Button Poetry, 2026), examines the long shadows of a toxic relationship and the aftermath of sexual assault, weaving personal history with persona poems that explore power, trauma and reclamation. Her writing has been featured in *Frontier Poetry, TRASH MAG, Ink and Marrow, Anti-Heroin Chic* and elsewhere.

Beyond the page, Aly is a lover of fantasy novels, licorice root tea and admiring the birds that visit her back porch. She lives with her husband, two cats and dog. Find her on Instagram at @_AlyAcevedo_.

author book recommendations

Shapeshifter by L.E. Bowman

Shapeshifter is a quiet hand on your shoulder, a mirror held gently to your becoming. L.E. Bowman writes like a friend who sees you—through struggle, gratitude and the soft edges of confusion. Each poem nudges you inward, and by the final page, you don't just understand yourself better—you feel a little less alone in the knowing.

Ephemera by Sierra DeMulder

Ephemera is the book I return to when I am lost in grief or brimming with hope. A quiet reminder that all we love is fragile, that we must hold it close because we never know when it will slip away. Sierra carries us through loss, joy and heartbreak, only to leave us standing in the hush of a passing moment, wondering if we held it tightly enough.

Home.Girl.Hood by Ebony Stewart

Home.Girl.Hood. is unashamed, fierce and unflinching. A celebration of all things woman—seen, unseen, silenced, yet never lost. Ebony writes to empower, to uplift, to build. She speaks to her community with love and truth, and in doing so, leaves every reader with a deeper sense of understanding, solidarity and pride.

credits

Assistant Editors

Sierra DeMulder
Charley Eatchel
Isabelle Keller
Alix Wolf

Book Photography

Emily Van Cook

Cover and Interior Design

Victoria Alvarez
Alix Wolf

Distribution

SCB Distributors

Ebook Production

Siva Ram Maganti

Publisher

Sam Van Cook

Publishing Operations Manager

TaneshaNicole Kozler

Publishing Operations Assistant

Charley Eatchel

Social Media and Marketing

Nancy Nguyen
Eric Tu

other books by button poetry

If you enjoyed this book, please consider checking out some of our others, below. Readers like you allow us to keep broadcasting and publishing. Thank you!

Darius Simpson, *Never Catch Me*
Blythe Baird, *Sweet, Young, & Worried*
Siaara Freeman, *Urbanshee*
Robert Wood Lynn, *How to Maintain Eye Contact*
Junious 'Jay' Ward, *Composition*
Usman Hameedi, *Staying Right Here*
Sean Patrick Mulroy, *Hated for the Gods*
Sierra DeMulder, *Ephemera*
Taylor Mali, *Poetry By Chance*
Matt Coonan, *Toy Gun*
Matt Mason, *Rock Stars*
Miya Coleman, *Cottonmouth*
Ty Chapman, *Tartarus*
Lara Coley, *ex traction*
DeShara Suggs-Joe, *If My Flowers Bloom*
Ollie Schminkey, *Where I Dry the Flowers*
Edythe Rodriguez, *We, The Spirits*
Topaz Winters, *Portrait of My Body as a Crime I'm Still Committing*
Zach Goldberg, *I'd Rather Be Destroyed*
Eric Sirota, *The Rent Eats First*
Neil Hilborn, *About Time*
Josh Tvrdy, *Smut Psalm*
Phil SaintDenisSanchez, *before & after our bodies*
Ebony Stewart, *WASH*
L.E. Bowman, *Shapeshifter*
Najya Williams, *on a date with disappointment*
Jalen Eutsey, *Bubble Gum Stadium*
Meg Ford, *Wild/Hurt*
Jared Singer, *Forgotten Necessities*
Daniel Elias Galicia, *Still Desert*
Chelsea Guevara, *Cipota*
Mickie Kennedy, *Glandscapes*
FreeQuency, *(On /Un-)Becoming*
Hailey Tran, *an everyday occurrence*
Kristina Percy, *Both True*
Gigi Bella, *without the frills*

Available at buttonpoetry.com/shop and more!